SEA ANIMALS

Pat Stewart

DOVER PUBLICATIONS, INC.
Mineola, New York

Bibliographical Note

Sea Animals is a new work, first published by Dover Publications, Inc., in 1999.

International Standard Book Number: 0-486-40558-3

Manufactured in the United States of America
Dover Publications, Inc., 31 East 2nd Street, Mineola, N.Y. 11501

Dolphins dive in and out of the water.

Every winter, this humpback whale swims from
Alaska to Hawaii.

The swordfish is a swift and powerful swimmer.

The inside of the conch shell is shiny pink.

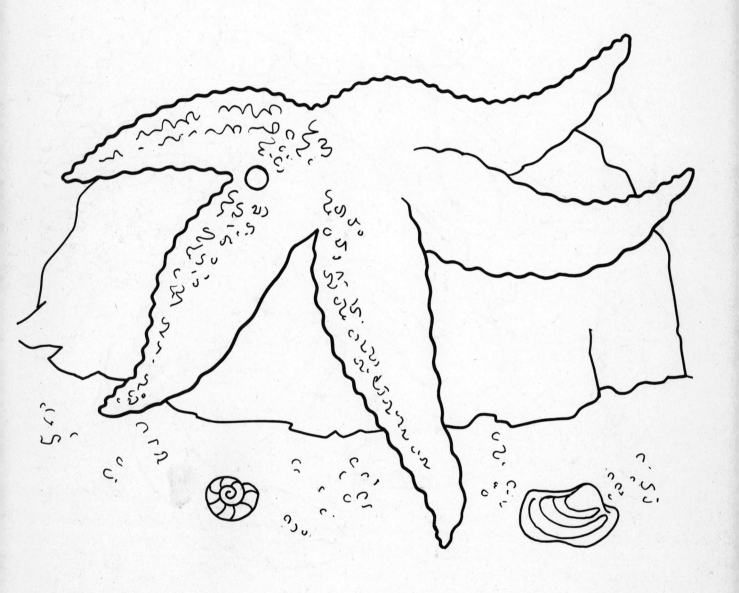

The starfish hunts for snails and clams by
digging through the sand with its pointed feet.

Blue crabs swim in bays and streams.

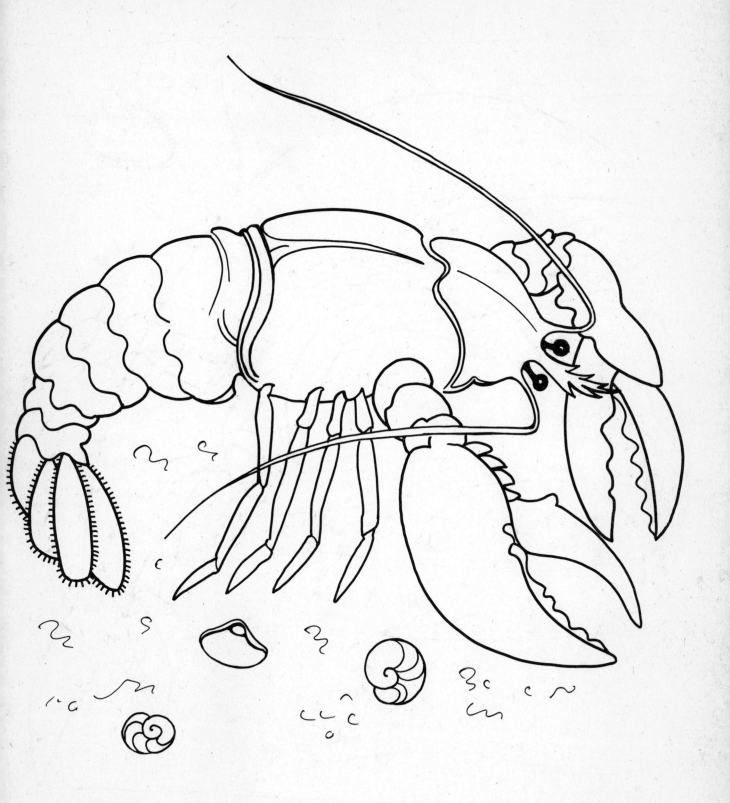

For many people, eating lobster
is a special treat.

The great white shark hunts for seals
and turtles to eat.

The manta ray has eyes on each side
of its head.

The walrus has two long, white tusks.

The killer whale has a tall dorsal fin
in the middle of its back.

The sea lion is a very large seal.

The sea turtle has feet like paddles.

The manatee swims so slowly,
sometimes it is injured by fast moving boats.

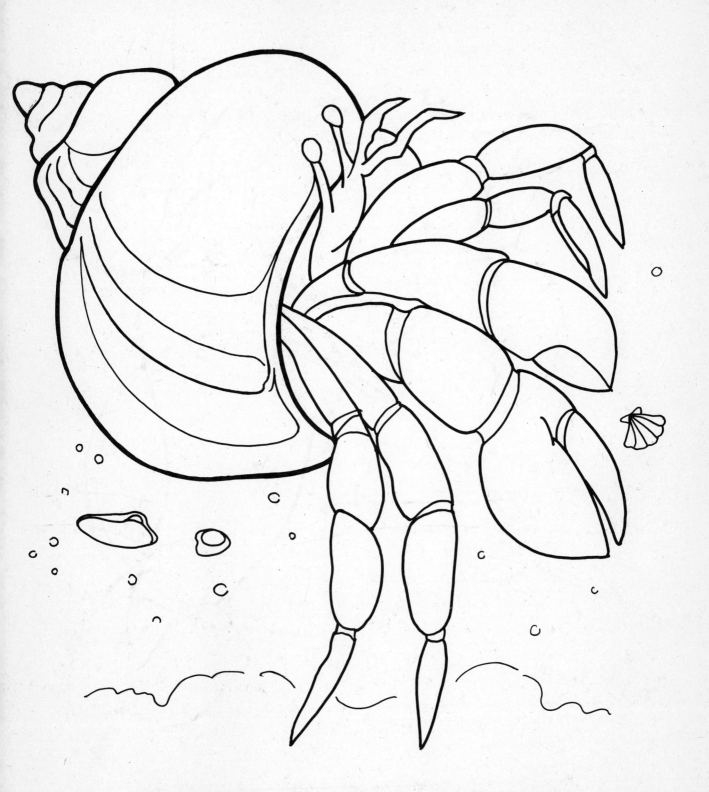

As the hermit crab grows, it moves into larger and larger shells which have been abandoned by snails.

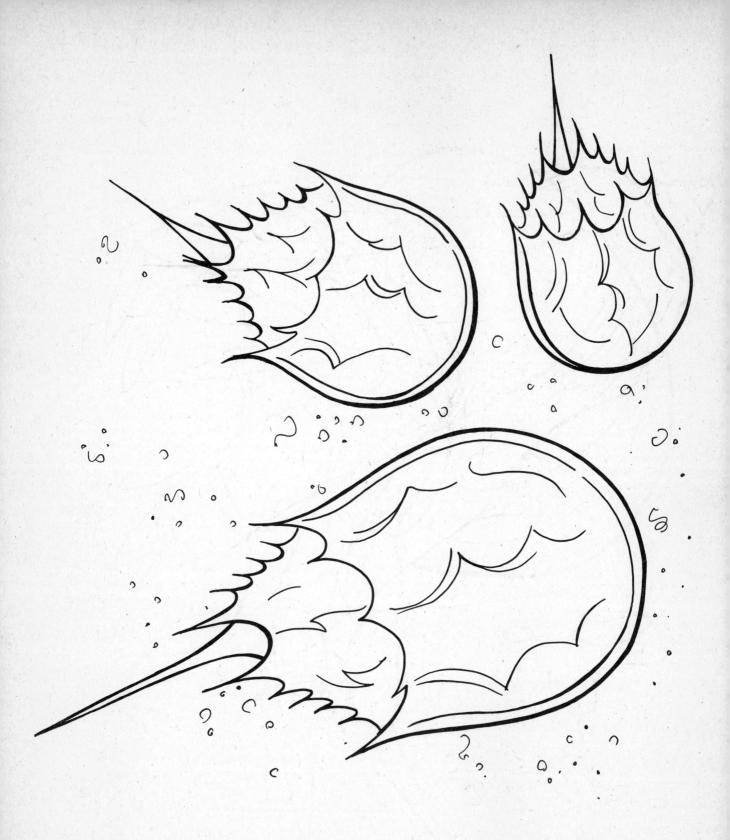

Horseshoe crabs live on the sandy bottoms
of shallow waters.

Barracudas have very sharp teeth.

The sailfish is one of the fastest fish in the sea.

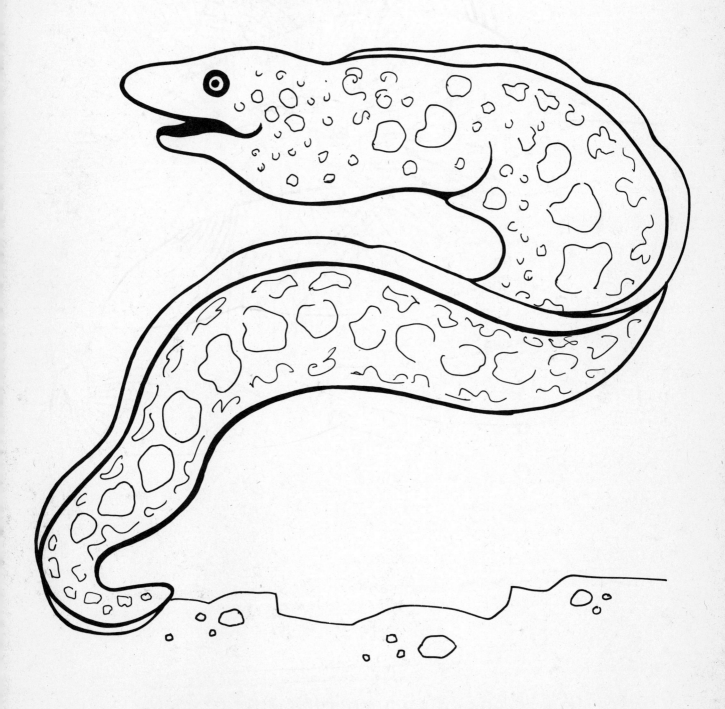

The moray eel likes to eat at night.

The shells of sea urchins are covered
with pointy spines.

The tentacles of the Portuguese
man-of-war have a powerful sting.

The octopus has 8 arms.

Shrimp help keep the water clean
by eating dirt from the bottom of the sea.

The giant squid can grow to be 60 feet long.

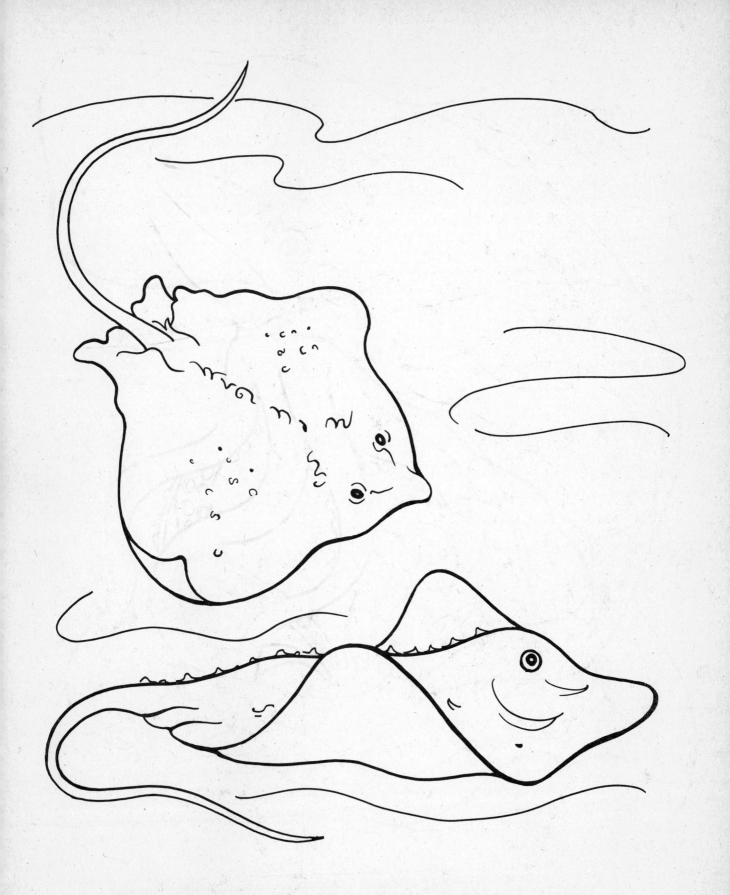

The stingray glides gracefully through
the water.

The sperm whale can dive deeper
than any other marine mammal.

Seals, with their webbed flippers
and warm fur, love to swim in cold water.

The sea anemone has long tentacles
that look like fingers.

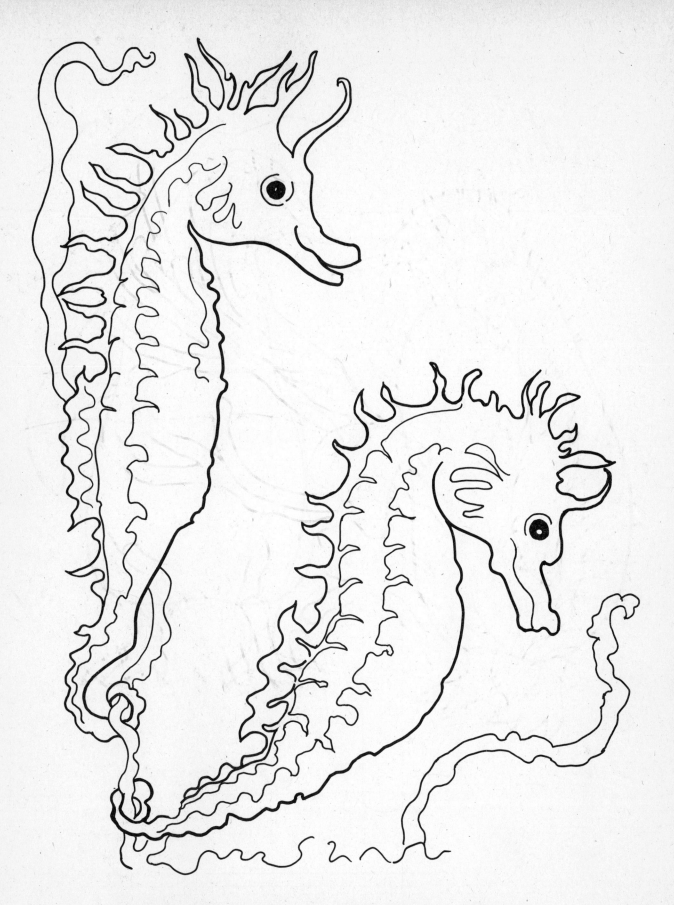

Seahorses use their tails to attach
themselves to plants.

Penguins are birds that can't fly,
but they swim very well.